THE BASICS OF MINISTRY SERIES

Guide for the Assembly by Cardinal Joseph Bernardin
Guide for Sunday Mass: Gather Faithfully Together
    by Cardinal Roger Mahony
Guide to Keeping Sunday Holy: Apostolic Letter Dies Domini
    by Pope John Paul II
Guide for Lectors by Aelred Rosser
Guide for Ushers and Greeters by Lawrence E. Mick
Guide for Sponsors by Ron Lewinski
Guide to the Revised Lectionary by Martin Connell

Video Guide for Gather Faithfully Together
Video Guide for Ministers of Communion

Guía para la Asamblea por Cardenal Joseph Bernardin
Guía para la Misa Dominical: Reúnanse Fielmente en Asamblea por Cardenal
    Roger Mahony
Guía para la Santificación del Domingo: Carta Apostólica Dies Domini
    por Su Santidad Juan Pablo II
Guía para los diáconos en la liturgia por Richard Vega
El Privilegio de Ser Padrino o Madrina: Guía para Patrocinadores del
    Catecumenado, traducción y adaptación por Pedro Rodriguez

Video Guía para Reúnanse Fielmente en Asamblea
Video Guía para Ministros de Comunión

GUIDE FOR MINISTERS OF COMMUNION

Victoria M. Tufano

LITURGY
TRAINING
PUBLICATIONS

ACKNOWLEDGMENTS

Excerpts from the English translation of *Pastoral Care of the Sick: Rites of Anointing and Viaticum* © 1982 International Committee on English in the Liturgy, Inc. All rights reserved.

Scripture excerpts are taken from the *New American Bible* © 1970 Confraternity of Christian Doctrine, Inc., Washington, DC. Used with permission. All rights reserved. No part of the *New American Bible* may be reproduced by any means without permission in writing from the copyright owner.

Excerpts from *Book of Blessings, additional blessings for use in the United States* © 1988 Confraternity of Christian Doctrine, Inc., Washington, DC. Used with permission. All rights reserved.

Excerpts from the Spanish translation of *Cuidado Pastoral de los Enfermos: Ritos de la Unción y del Viático* © 1984 Obra Nacional de la Buena Prensa, A.C. All rights reserved.

GUIDE FOR MINISTERS OF COMMUNION © 1999 Archdiocese of Chicago: Liturgy Training Publications, 1800 North Hermitage Avenue, Chicago IL 60622-1101; 1-800-933-1800; orders@ltp.org; fax 1-800-933-7094. All rights reserved.

Visit our website at www.ltp.org.

David A. Lysik was the editor of this book. Bryan Cones was the production editor. Anna Manhart designed the *Basics of Ministry* series, and Kari Nicholls typeset this volume in Goudy. It was printed by Metro Litho of Oak Forest, Illinois. Cover photo and photos on pages 23 and 39 are by Antonio Pérez; photos on pages i and 33 are by Bill Wittman; photos on pages 2, 4, 8 and 15 are by Eileen Crowley-Horak.

03 02 01 00   5 4 3 2

ISBN 1-56854-236-4

EGCOM

CONTENTS

Welcome!

If you are reading this book, you are most likely a minister of communion or are training to become one. In either case, you have heard the call to serve God's people in a particular way and have responded to that call.

The purpose of this book is to help you deepen your appreciation of the importance and dignity of the ministry you have undertaken. The practical issues surrounding both your role in the communion rite of the Mass and your task of bringing communion to the sick or homebound will be discussed, but always with the understanding that what you do as a minister of communion is more than a mere function or job that could be done by any available person.

As a minister of communion you are first and foremost a member of the body of Christ, one of the holy people of God. In baptism you were claimed by Christ as one of his own and marked with the sign of his cross. Through the waters of baptism you died with Christ to all that was not of God and were cleansed of all that could separate you from God. In confirmation you were anointed with chrism as one who shares in the priestly, prophetic and royal ministry of Jesus, the anointed one, the Christ.

In your life as a Christian you have lived out that ministry in many ways. In your home, in your place of work and in your relationships in the parish and the local community, you have carried on the work of Jesus by trying to live as he lived and taught. However, the fullest and most central expression of your ministry as a baptized Christian has been your participation in the celebration of the eucharist.

Week by week and year by year, for nearly 20 centuries, the holy baptized people of God have exercised the priestly, prophetic and royal ministry of Jesus. In the Mass the presence of Christ proclaimed in the scriptures deepens our faith and stirs our hearts to carry out that ministry. The one who preaches exercises a prophetic ministry, speaking to us the truth that God would have us hear, that we might speak and live that truth in our own lives. Just as Christ the high priest intercedes with the Father for all of creation, we lift up the needs of the world and the church in the prayers of the faithful. In the great prayer of thanks and praise, the eucharistic prayer, we take our part in the sacrifice that Christ eternally offers to God the Father through the power of the Holy Spirit. That same Christ, truly present in the bread and wine that we offer to God, is given to us by God as food and drink, as strength and nourishment, so that we may be dismissed from the liturgy to carry on the work of Jesus: the proclamation of the good news of salvation and the reconciliation of the world to God in Christ.

As a baptized Christian, you are already participating fully and deeply in the ministry of Jesus. As a minister of communion, you are called on to serve the body of Christ, the church, as it performs its most important work — the eucharist. Like all ministry, this is a great honor and a great responsibility. Undertake it with the intention to grow in your devotion to the Mass, to the church that celebrates it, and to the Lord, through whom, with whom and in whom it can be done.

Questions for Reflection and Discussion

1. What started you on the path to become a minister of communion? Were you asked? By whom? Did you hesitate or have to think it over? Why did you finally accept? Did you volunteer? Why? What was the response to your offer?

2. If you are a new minister, what are your questions, concerns or fears as you prepare?

3. If you are an experienced minister, what would you tell someone who is preparing to become, or is considering becoming, a minister of communion?

4. Would you say the Lord called you to this ministry? If so, how do you know that?

5. How does baptism put us into relationship with other members of the church? How does the ministry of communion flow from our baptism?

6. Have you ever related the table where you share meals with friends and family to the table of the Lord at the eucharist? What do you bring from your table to the Lord's table? From the Lord's table to your table?

What Is a Minister of Communion?

Since the beginning of the church's history, Christians have gathered on Sunday to hear and proclaim the scriptures, to collect gifts for the poor, to pray for the living and the dead, to offer thanks and praise, to recognize Christ present in the breaking of the bread and the sharing of the cup. This is a lot of work and takes a lot of people to accomplish. Much has to happen both before and after the gathering to make it all go smoothly. More importantly, the people who gather must strive to live in such a way that what happens at the gathering makes a difference in daily life.

A Historical Perspective

In the earliest years of the church, the many tasks surrounding the celebration of the eucharist and the consequences of that celebration were the concern of the whole community. Positions of leadership and ministry took decades to develop and even longer to solidify. Nowhere in any of the writings of the early church is the phrase "minister of communion" to be found, but there are descriptions of ordinary Christians bringing the presence of Christ in the consecrated bread of the eucharist to others.

When the church gathered, the members did not feel complete if anyone was missing. Those who were absent because they were sick or imprisoned (why else would anyone stay away?) were certainly remembered in prayer. Family members or others would take the body of Christ from the gathering to those who were absent. This was not a casual act. In many places Christians gathered at the risk of their lives. The authorities considered Christianity to be a threat to the good order of society (and probably to the authorities' own power). Taking part in Christian worship was grounds for arrest, imprisonment, torture or execution. Being in possession of the eucharist carried the same consequences.

One account that we have of people taking communion to those who were absent from the gathering comes from Saint Justin, a second-century martyr who tried to explain Christian beliefs and practices in a written account called *The First Apology*. ("Apology" here means "sympathetic explanation" rather than being sorry.) Writing in approximately the year 150, Justin explains:

> On the day which is called Sunday, all, whether they live in the town or in the country, gather in the same place. Then the memoirs of the apostles or the writings of the prophets are read for as long as time allows. When the reader has finished, the president speaks, exhorting us to live by these noble teachings. Then we rise together and pray. Then . . . when the prayer is finished, bread, wine and water are brought. The president then prays and gives thanks as well as he can. And all the people reply with the

acclamation "Amen!" After this, the gifts are distributed and shared out to everyone, and those serving take them to those who are absent.

The best known story of a Christian risking his life to bring the eucharist to others is that of Tarcissus (sometimes called Tarsicius). Not much is known of him other than this: While he was carrying the eucharist, a mob of unbelievers confronted him and asked him what he was carrying. When he would not surrender the blessed sacrament to them, they beat him to death. Legend has it that Tarcissus was a young boy bringing the eucharist to those in prison, although he may have been an acolyte or deacon. Whatever the details, he was a "minister of communion" who understood the depth of his ministry.

Extraordinary Ministers of Communion

As the various ministries of the church developed over the centuries, the ministry of distributing the body of Christ and ensuring its secure reservation became the responsibility of the clergy. Until the 1970s, except in the most dire circumstances (usually nothing short of war), only a bishop, priest or deacon could minister the eucharist. Bishops, priests and deacons are "ordinary" ministers of communion, meaning that the ministry of communion is considered a usual, intrinsic part of their role in the church.

In 1965 Pope Paul VI began to grant permission for others to minister communion in very specific circumstances. At first, certain religious sisters and brothers were granted permission to distribute communion in the chapels of their religious houses when a priest or deacon was unavailable. Soon individual bishops were asking for such permission for lay people in their dioceses, and national bishops' conferences were asking permission for their countries. In 1973, in a document called *Immensae caritatis* (Latin for "of boundless charity"), Paul VI approved giving each bishop the authority to mandate religious sisters and brothers and laity to administer communion so that "access to communion may be made easier, so that by sharing more fully in the effects of the sacrifice of the Mass, the faithful may more willingly and intensely give themselves to God and to the good of the church and all humanity."

In that document Paul VI explicitly affirms that ministers of communion may serve

> within Mass because of a great crowd of people or some disability of the celebrant [and] outside Mass when distance makes it difficult to bring communion especially as viaticum to the sick in danger of death; or when the sheer number of sick people, especially in hospitals or similar institutions, requires several ministers.

Because the ministry of communion was not considered an ordinary, intrinsic part of these religious and lay ministers' roles, they were sometimes called "extraordinary" — outside the ordinary — ministers of communion. Many parishes still use this term.

Questions for Reflection and Discussion

1. What types of preparation must take place before the community can celebrate the eucharist?

2. How does one live in such a way that participation in the eucharistic gathering makes a difference in daily life?

3. Do we still have a sense that we are incomplete as a church when some are missing from the eucharist? If so, how do we express it? If not, how might we recapture that sense?

4. How might Tarcissus' example inspire ministers of communion today?

5. In what ways do you consider ministers of communion to be "extraordinary"?

Qualities of a Minister of Communion

What qualities should a minister of communion bring to this ministry? Paul VI's 1973 instruction *Immensae caritatis* notes:

> The faithful who are special ministers of communion must be persons whose good qualities of Christian life, faith and morals recommend them. Let them strive to be worthy of this great office, foster their own devotion to the eucharist, and show an example to the rest of the faithful by their own devotion and reverence toward the most august sacrament of the altar.

What are the "good qualities of Christian life"? Individual ministers bring their own unique qualities with them to the ministry of communion. Some of these good qualities are pure gift, a matter of personality and temperament. Others have been developed through discipline, experience and struggle. When these good qualities are brought to the ministry of communion, both the qualities and the ministry are enhanced.

As the ministry of communion matures and deepens within individuals, it may lead them to focus on certain qualities that they may wish to develop or refine within themselves. For each person this will be different. Ministers of communion may find it helpful to keep a journal, to develop a relationship with a spiritual director or a wise friend, or to join with other ministers of communion to reflect on the effect their ministry is having. While each minister will bring or develop different qualities, reflections on four particular ones are offered here as examples.

Humility

As *Immensae caritatis* notes, being a minister of communion is a "great office." It is an honor, and one who has been chosen for the job should acknowledge that. But the honor should not cause the minister to have an exalted self-opinion. Jesus, the role model for all ministry, taught his disciples that ministry was about service. To make the point absolutely clear, he put on an apron and washed their feet (see John 13:1 – 20). This created quite a stir among the disciples, and Peter, ever brash and outspoken, initally refused to let it be done to him.

What was Peter's objection? Did he object because his master was acting in the role of servant? Or was it because he knew that whatever role the Lord took on, his disciples would also be required to take on? Was it false humility that would not allow Peter to have his feet washed by his teacher, or false pride that would not accept the mandate to wash others' feet?

As ministers of communion, we are usually willing to do whatever is asked of us. We try to serve at liturgy whenever we are needed, and to travel to homes and hospitals where sick or homebound parishioners are. We gladly give the Lord to our brothers and sisters. Are we equally ready to accept the Lord from them?

As baptized members of the body of Christ, those to whom we minister the eucharist also have Christ present within them. Can we see, revere and accept Christ through them? Can we accept with joy and humility the many ways that Christ ministers to us, even while he ministers through us?

Hospitality

One of the most disturbing aspects of Jesus' ministry to the people of his time was his eagerness and willingness to share a meal with anyone at any time. In the Middle Eastern culture of Jesus' day, meals were regimented ways of acknowledging who was superior to whom. The structure of society was reflected, and in many ways maintained, by who ate with whom.

Jesus was not interested in maintaining the structures of human society, but was instead interested in teaching us about relationships in God's society. Where God reigns, all are welcome. Everyone has a place at God's table. The mission of Jesus was to bring the whole world to God's table, to restore the unity of creation that sin had destroyed. That mission is handed on to every baptized member of the church.

When we celebrate the eucharist, we eat and drink at the table of the Lord in anticipation of the day when all will do the same. In one sense, the eucharist is a rehearsal for the heavenly banquet. We get to "try out" our heavenly table manners. At the banquet of the Lord, all are equal. There is no head table. There is no children's table. There is no servants' table. The same is true of the eucharist. All who gather are honored guests.

As ministers of communion, we too are honored guests. But we are also appointed servants. Our task is to welcome those who approach the Lord's table, to extend to them the same hospitality that has been extended to us.

In the brief encounter that we have with each person to whom we minister at the liturgy, it may seem difficult to convey much to anyone. But a posture that is both attentive and relaxed, a warm smile, eye contact, an unhurried but efficient pace, a tone of voice that is reverent and cordial, all convey hospitality. These things take time to develop as the minister becomes more experienced and at ease. But from the beginning, every minister should approach the task with an attitude of hospitality.

Gratitude

The sacrament whose ministry is our special care is the *eucharist*, which comes from the Greek word for "thanks." The ordinary way of saying "thank you" in modern Greece is *eucharisto*, just as it was in the time of Jesus.

The giving of thanks and praise in the eucharist is the central and essential action of the church. For what do we give thanks and praise? First and foremost for Jesus Christ, in whom all things are created and redeemed. As people baptized into Christ, we offer thanks for all of creation, for all that is good; in the words of Eucharistic Prayer III, for "all life, all holiness."

In the liturgy we constantly read and tell the stories of how God has acted through and on behalf of humanity, especially through the Jewish people and through the church. The church calls this "salvation history." We keep God's action before us always so that we may be grateful, but also so that we may be hopeful. The God who has always been attentive and faithful to us in the past will not abandon us. For this reason we can face the future with confidence that God will always be with us.

The gratitude that we express in the eucharist is a basic element of each individual's life, too. Each of us has a "salvation history," a story of how God has always walked with us, acting through us and for us. Our response to that personal story is also one of gratitude and hope. We must never forget how God has been active in our lives; we must tell our stories and listen to the stories of others. A grateful heart has no room for self-pity or envy. Grateful persons share their gifts and blessings with others and receive the gifts and blessings that others have to share. We must receive the great gift of the Lord's presence with grateful hearts and share that gift generously and joyfully with others, both in the ministry of communion and in our daily lives.

Reverence

As Catholics, we have been taught since our earliest days to treat the presence of the Lord in the eucharist with the utmost reverence. How we walk and hold our bodies as we receive the body and the blood of Christ, the gestures that we make as we pass the tabernacle or the church, the beauty of the place where the sacrament is reserved, the flame that announces the presence of the Lord: All these were taught to us as ways to express our reverence.

As ministers of communion, we are teachers of reverence. How we act as we approach the altar, how we handle the sacred species of bread and wine, how we dress to perform our ministry, not only express our own attitudes but also form the attitudes of others.

The reverence that we owe to the presence of Christ in the eucharist we also owe to the scriptures, the gathered assembly and the priest, because, as the *Constitution on the Sacred Liturgy* (#7) of the Second Vatican Council notes, Christ is also present in them. All Catholics must be attentive and reverent to the many ways Christ is present; as teachers of reverence, ministers of communion must be especially so.

Our attentiveness to the scriptures as they are proclaimed in the assembly must be matched by the same attentiveness in our personal reading and study of scripture. We must listen deeply for the voice of the Lord in these readings, for the presence of the

Lord speaking to our hearts, to our families, to our parish and to our community.

Just as we would never harm the body of anyone we love, we must care for the body of Christ that is the church. This would seem to go without saying. Who among us would purposely injure the church? But our most real and ordinary contacts with the church are those with are our fellow parishioners, the people who sit around us at Mass each Sunday. A character in the *Peanuts* comic strip once said, "I love mankind; it's people I can't stand." But we cannot say, "I love the church; it's parishioners I can't stand." Saint John says it more strongly: "Those who say, 'I love God,' and hate their brothers or sisters, are liars" (1 John 4:20, NRSV).

In our parish, as in any group of human beings, there may be individuals we find difficult to deal with, people whose opinions are at odds with our own, and people who are so different from us that we cannot begin to understand them. There may also be committees or other groups of people who espouse ways of doing things that we feel we must oppose. This is a human reality. The deeper, spiritual reality is that these people are one with us in the body of Christ. We may disagree with them or oppose their ideas, but we may not speak ill of them or tear the community apart over any issue. We must have reverence for the people who are the body of Christ.

The same is true of our clergy and other pastoral leaders. In their ministry of leadership and prayer, they are the presence of Christ to us. We owe them the same reverence that we owe Christ; they owe that same reverence to the people.

Questions for Reflection and Discussion

1. What "good qualities of Christian life" do you bring to the ministry of communion?

2. If you are an experienced minister, has this ministry uncovered any new qualities or deepened those you have always recognized? If so, which qualities? How have they been uncovered or deepened?

3. Reflect on the four qualities discussed in this chapter: humility, hospitality, gratitude and reverence. In what ways do you see these qualities in yourself? In your daily life? In your ministry? How would you nurture these qualities in yourself?

4. What other qualities do you think that ministers of communion should develop or deepen in themselves?

Ministering Communion at Mass

The procedures for the ministry of communion at Mass begin long before the Mass itself.

Schedules

Every minister of communion is responsible for serving when scheduled. Courtesy and common sense dictate that a minister notify the appropriate person or find a substitute when he or she is unable to serve at a scheduled time. Ministers should also notify the person who makes the schedule if they will be out of town for a period of time or if they will be unable to serve at a particular liturgy each week.

Many parishes provide the ministers of communion with a schedule for a month or a quarter or a season. When your schedule arrives, mark the dates and times on your personal calendar and, if necessary, on the family calendar. If you know right away that you cannot serve for one or more times that you are scheduled, contact the coordinator immediately or find a substitute.

If assignments are made by phone, be sure to have your calendar open when you are speaking to the coordinator. If your calendar is not at hand, write down the dates and check them as soon as possible. Either call the coordinator back if you find that you have a conflict, or find a substitute.

A list of active ministers of communion and their telephone numbers is a very helpful tool when seeking a substitute. E-mail addresses and fax numbers might also be useful.

Illness

If a minister of communion has the flu, a cold or other illness that can be spread easily, it is far more thoughtful to the community to find a substitute than to risk spreading illness by handling what others will eat and drink. During cold season, it may also be advisable for the parish to put a friendly reminder in the parish bulletin that all who are suffering from a cold should receive only the eucharistic bread until they have recovered.

Just before the Liturgy

Many parishes that have several ministers of communion at each Mass have a procedure for signing in. If this is so in your parish, arrive ten or fifteen minutes before the scheduled time of Mass and follow the procedure. Be sure to find out what communion station you are assigned to and if there are any special circumstances you should know about.

In a parish that uses only one or two ministers at each Mass, a sign-in procedure may not be necessary, but it is still a courtesy to let the presider or sacristan know that you are there. The presider may not know who is assigned to minister at that Mass, and knowing that you are there and ready is one less thing for him to be concerned about.

Some parishes ask that ministers of communion who are not assigned to serve at the liturgy they are attending go to the sacristy or other place where the sign-in takes place to see if they might be needed. This may be especially helpful during the summer or school breaks, when many families leave town and a minister may have forgotten to arrange for a substitute.

As the Liturgy Begins

In most parishes, the ministers of communion sit in the assembly until it is time for them to perform their ministry. Many find it helpful to try to sit near the end of a row so they do not have to disturb people to get out, although this is not always possible.

Some parishes have the ministers participate in the entrance procession. This practice makes the procession larger and more diverse, and it helps "count noses" to see if enough ministers are present or if there is a need for volunteers. If the ministers are to be in the procession, they should be there on time. In some parishes, all the ministers serving in the liturgy pray together just before the procession begins.

A few parishes provide seating for ministers of communion in the sanctuary or near the front of the assembly, although most ministers prefer to sit with their families and the rest of the worshiping community.

Whatever the practice in your parish, follow it. If you have suggestions for changing the procedure, make them courteously and in writing to the appropriate person. Do not change a procedure on your own.

During the Communion Rite

Each parish has its own plan for the distribution of communion. What follows here is only a general outline. Write your parish's procedure on the page allotted at the end of this book, or keep a printed copy of the procedure with this book.

The Sign of Peace

In most parishes, ministers of communion remain in their places long enough to exchange the sign of peace with those near them. They then proceed, without haste but efficiently, to the area near the altar. Additional cups and plates or baskets may be brought to the altar from a side table at this time.

The Breaking of the Bread and the Pouring of the Wine

The ministers break the bread and pour the wine during the singing of the "Lamb of God." Ministers may assist the priest (and deacon, if one is present) in breaking the consecrated bread and dividing it among the additional plates or baskets, and in pouring the consecrated wine into the additional cups. Follow your parish's procedure or the direction of the priest or deacon.

During this time, only those who are preparing the consecrated elements for distribution should be moving. Other ministers of communion should stand still, facing the altar. Unnecessary movement will distract the assembly from the action that is taking place at the altar. Although the breaking of the bread and the pouring of the wine may seem to be purely practical activities, they stand at the heart of what the eucharist is about: Christ's very self, broken and poured out for us, the unity of the many in the one bread and one cup. Our ancestors in the faith found this so important that they sometimes referred to the entire liturgy as "the breaking of the bread."

The consecrated elements should be treated with care. If the breaking and pouring are done at a reverent pace, the risk of spilling or dropping anything is minimized.

The Invitation to Communion

After all the cups and plates are prepared, a plate and cup are raised so that all may see, and the presider gives the invitation to communion. Again, no one should be moving during this action.

The Distribution of Communion

In each parish, how communion ministers themselves receive communion and how they receive the vessels containing the consecrated elements for distribution varies.

Once the minister of communion is in place, he or she gives full attention to each person who comes forward, greeting each communicant with a direct gaze and a pleasant expression.

Ministers offer the consecrated bread by holding up one piece to the communicant's view, looking into the eyes of the communicant, and saying clearly, "The body of Christ." The minister waits until he or she responds, "Amen." The communicant then holds out cupped hands, or opens the mouth and extends the tongue.

Receiving communion on the tongue or in the hand is the choice of the one receiving. If you are giving communion in the hand, place the consecrated bread firmly in the palm of the person's hand. If the person prefers to receive on the tongue, place the bread so that it rests entirely on the tongue if possible. Try not to touch the tongue with your fingers. You may wish to have a tissue or a finger towel in your pocket or in the hand that is holding the plate or basket in case you need to wipe your fingers.

Ministers offer the blood of Christ by holding up the cup to the communicant's view, looking into the eyes of the communicant, and saying clearly, "The blood of Christ." The minister waits until he or she responds, "Amen." The communicant then takes the cup and drinks a small amount. (Do not try to tip the cup toward the person's mouth. This is more likely to cause an accident than handing the cup to the person.)

The minister then receives the cup back from the person with both hands, wiping the rim of the cup inside and out with a purificator where the person drank, and removing any lipstick or lip balm to the extent possible. The minister turns the cup about a quarter turn before presenting it to the next person so that he or she will drink from a different spot than the previous communicant.

Persons Needing Assistance

Persons who tremble due to illness or age may need some assistance drinking from the cup, or they may steady themselves by placing a hand on your arm or shoulder. Accept the gesture graciously, and be ready to offer further assistance if necessary.

Blind persons will need assistance locating the cup. Help them by taking their hand and placing it firmly on the cup. They will then drink without assistance and hold the cup out for you to receive it.

Children may need to be encouraged to take the cup in both hands. Do this quietly and politely.

In some parishes, as the communion procession begins, ushers direct the priest or minister of communion to persons with wheelchairs or crutches. Ushers should be sure to ask such persons when they enter the church if this is what they would prefer; they might prefer to participate in the communion procession.

When offering communion to a person in a wheelchair, it may be more graceful and polite to sit or kneel, or at least to stoop, rather than to tower over them. It may also be considerate to offer communion to the person's companion at that time.

After Communion

When all have received communion, the ministers make sure that their vessels are brought to the proper places. If any of the consecrated bread remains after communion, it should be brought to the tabernacle. This is done simply, without attracting attention.

It is appropriate that only one minister go to the tabernacle, unless several full vessels of bread need to be reserved. If the bread used for communion will become stale if stored, the procedure for consuming the remaining wine should be followed.

If any of the blood of Christ remains after communion, it should be consumed by the ministers in a reverent and unobtrusive manner. If a large amount of wine remains, it should be placed in the tabernacle (or another designated place where it will be safe) until the end of Mass.

Ministers should return to their seats and offer silent thanksgiving or participate in the post-communion hymn. If the ministers are delayed in the sacristy until the prayer after communion begins, they should remain in the sacristy, attentive to the liturgy, until the Mass ends.

After Mass

If a large amount of the body or blood of Christ remains after communion, ministers should gather in the sacristy or other appropriate place after Mass and consume what is left. Ministers may ask other members of the assembly to assist if there are not enough ministers to drink the remaining wine. While this is being done, a quiet and reverent atmosphere should be maintained.

Ministers may also be asked to help clean and put away the vessels for the next liturgy. If a vessel has been damaged and should be repaired or disposed of, the minister should bring it to the attention of the sacristan, ministry coordinator or priest.

Further Formation

The following books and videos offer further information on the role of the minister of communion during Mass and the celebration of the eucharist as a whole. They are all available from Liturgy Training Publications.

Video Guide for Ministers of Communion. This video offers a visual presentation of the practical tasks of communion ministry during Mass. It also includes comments on communion ministry by the ministers themselves.

The Communion Rite at Sunday Mass by Gabe Huck. This book considers all aspects of the communion rite, in which ministers of communion participate in a unique way.

Guide for Sunday Mass: Gather Faithfully Together by Cardinal Roger Mahony. This pastoral letter by the archbishop of Los Angeles offers a detailed vision of a well-celebrated parish liturgy. Also available as a video.

A Eucharist Sourcebook. This collection of scripture, prayer and quotations from many sources is a resource for the spirituality of a minister of communion.

Babette's Feast. This feature-length film about a chef who serves in the house of two elderly sisters explores the deepest meanings of meal-sharing and service at table.

Ministering Communion
to the Sick or Homebound

The faithful who are ill are deprived of their rightful and accustomed place in the eucharistic community. In bringing communion to them the minister of communion represents Christ and manifests faith and charity on behalf of the whole community toward those who cannot be present at the eucharist. For the sick the reception of communion is not only a privilege but also a sign of support and concern shown by the Christian community for its members who are ill. (*Pastoral Care of the Sick*, 73)

A minister of communion who brings the blessed sacrament to a sick or homebound person ministers to the body of Christ in many ways.

First, the minister is a representative of the praying community to someone who is unable to take his or her place within it. The minister carries not only the precious body and blood of Christ in the eucharistic elements; he or she also carries the love, prayers and concerns of the body of Christ, the church, to one of its members.

Second, the minister is entrusted with the reverent and safe transport of the consecrated bread and, on rare occasions, the consecrated wine.

Third, the minister serves the suffering body of Christ in the person of the one to whom they bring communion. Mother Teresa of Calcutta often said that she served the poor and suffering because she saw Christ in them. Ministers of communion do well to see Christ in those to whom they minister.

Fourth, the minister brings Christ to the sick or homebound in the minister's own person, as well as in the eucharist.

Fifth, ministers may bring back to the larger community the needs of the sick person. If the community can provide material goods or volunteer help, or if the parish's ministers can help the person receive needed medical attention or government benefits, or if the parish priest should be alerted that the person wishes to celebrate the sacrament of penance or of anointing of the sick, the minister of communion can make the need known.

Preparations

Ministering communion to a sick person is much more than simply delivering the blessed sacrament. It is a time of prayer structured very much like the Mass, which means that both the minister and the person receiving communion should prepare for the visit.

Time and Information

Call the place where the person you are visiting is — their home, a nursing home, the hospital — and speak with the person or their caregiver to arrange a time for your visit. Ideally, a communion minister would go directly from the Sunday liturgy to the communion visit, although this is not always possible.

Find out how sick the person is, if they are able to be out of bed, if they can tolerate an extended visit, and if they are able to swallow consecrated bread or a host. Find out if there are others who would also like to receive communion during your visit. Ask if items such as a candle and a plain white linen cloth are available. If necessary, get the address and directions.

Materials

The most important resources that a minister brings to a communion visit are the blessed sacrament and the minister himself or herself. But a minister will also want to have a few other items:

Scripture readings: The minister will want to have the scriptures of the day easily available. These might be marked in a Bible or in another resource, such as *At Home with the Word* or a parish worship aid.

Pyx: The container that is used to transport the consecrated bread is called a pyx. It is a small metal box, often decorated with an image related to the eucharist. Some come with a leather or cloth case. Some parishes have pyxes for use by ministers of communion; many ministers who visit the sick regularly have their own. They are available from Catholic religious goods stores and catalogs.

Table preparations: The ministers may wish to carry a clean, ironed white cloth (a linen napkin would do nicely), a candle and candle holder, a holy water container and matches.

Parish bulletin: The minister might bring the parish bulletin to help keep the person in touch with the larger community. Calendars and other materials from the parish are often greatly appreciated.

Preparing for the Visit

A minister may prepare for the visit in several ways. The best way is to participate in the Sunday eucharist before the visit. In this way, the minister has an opportunity to pray for the person to be visited, to hear and reflect on the scriptures, to offer thanks and praise to God, and to receive the body and blood of Christ.

As already mentioned, it may not be possible for the communion visit to take place right after Mass. In that case, the minister should still take time to read and reflect on the scriptures, to pray for the one who will be visited, to offer praise and thanks to God for all God's works great and small, and to ask God to work through him or her to bring Christ to the person the minister will visit.

The minister may also wish to review the rite of "Communion in Ordinary Circumstances" (provided in both English and Spanish as an appendix at the back of this book) and walk through it in his or her mind. It is important that the minister be at ease with the rite so that it can be celebrated well.

The Blessed Sacrament

The minister should obtain enough consecrated bread for all those who are anticipated to receive communion. This should be done just before the communion visit. The communion minister should not carry the blessed sacrament while engaged in other activities or errands.

If the communion visit will take place after Mass, the minister's pyx might be brought to the altar at the beginning of the communion rite so that the priest can place the bread in it. Some parishes have a dismissal and blessing of communion ministers after communion. In other parishes, the minister simply takes the filled pyx and carries it out after Mass.

If the communion visit will take place at another time, the minister will need to make arrangements to obtain the blessed sacrament. In some places, ministers who regularly take communion to the sick are told where the tabernacle key is kept so that they may take what they need whenever the church is unlocked. In this case, the minister should keep the location of the key confidential. In other parishes, the minister makes an appointment with the priest, deacon or sacristan.

In most cases, communion to the sick is given only in the form of bread. If the person has trouble swallowing, a small piece of the consecrated bread may be softened with water and ministered by spoon. It may be helpful to have a glass of water nearby.

If the sick person is unable to swallow solid food, a small amount of consecrated wine may be given. The precious blood should be carried in a sealed container, such as a pill bottle or a very small plastic food container. It may be administered by spoon or straw, or drunk from a glass.

The Visit

A general outline of "Communion in Ordinary Circumstances" follows below. Notice that the outline closely follows the structure of the Mass. Although the rite may seem stiff and formal, it can be used as a guide to shape a visit that is appropriate to each situation. If you are visiting one person, the visit can be less formal, but still prayerful. A situation in which there are several people, such as in a nursing home chapel, may require more formality.

INTRODUCTORY RITES
Greeting
Sprinkling with Holy Water
Penitential Rite

LITURGY OF THE WORD
Reading

Response

General Intercessions

LITURGY OF HOLY COMMUNION

The Lord's Prayer

Communion

Silent Prayer

Prayer after Communion

CONCLUDING RITE

Blessing

On the following pages, we will walk through a communion visit to one person who is not gravely ill and is able to take an active part in the visit.

Before the Service

When you enter the home or room of the person you are visiting, greet him or her in a warm, friendly manner. If necessary, introduce yourself and explain why you are there. Greet any others present, and, if it is appropriate, you may certainly chat for a few minutes before beginning the prayer. If you are a personal friend and are likely to have a lengthy and animated visit, it may be most appropriate to pray and minister communion early in the visit so that the presence of the blessed sacrament is not forgotten.

When the time comes to begin the prayer, the minister spreads out the cloth on the table, lights the candle, and sets the book with the scriptures on the table. The minister may sit in a chair next to or across from the sick person. If the person is in a high hospital bed, the minister may prefer to stand.

Introductory Rites

Everyone makes the sign of the cross, and the minister may offer a greeting such as, "The peace of the Lord be with you always," to which the other person replies, "And also with you." Then the minister places the pyx with the blessed sacrament on the cloth and opens it. A few moments of silence may follow. If it seems appropriate, the minister may sprinkle the person with holy water. A brief penitential rite follows. It may be a simple repetition of the Kyrie — "Lord, have mercy; Christ, have mercy; Lord, have mercy" — or the Confiteor from Mass ("I confess to almighty God . . ."). In some cases, a simple moment of silence to remember God's mercy may be sufficient.

Liturgy of the Word

One or more of the readings from the Mass may be read by the minister, the person who is ill, or anyone else who is present. The responsorial psalm may be prayed after the reading. The minister may offer some reflection on the reading, mention something that was said in the homily at the parish Mass, or engage the person in discussion about the reading. Some time for silent reflection may also be appropriate.

The minister may then offer some prayers of intercession like those in the Mass for the church, the world, the sick and others in need of prayer. The sick person and anyone else present may also be invited to do so.

Liturgy of Holy Communion

After all the intercessions have been made, everyone prays the Lord's Prayer. Then the minister takes the consecrated bread, holds it up and says, "This is the Lamb of God who takes away the sins of the world. Happy are those who are called to his supper," or something similar. All respond, "Lord, I am not worthy to receive you, but only say the word and I shall be healed."

The minister offers communion to everyone in the usual way. (Be aware that the sick person may need a sip of water to help swallow the communion bread.) A period of silence follows. The minister then offers a prayer. The following prayer from the rite, or one similar to it, may be used:

All-powerful God,
we thank you for the nourishment you give us
through your holy gift.
Pour out your Spirit upon us
and in the strength of this food from heaven
keep us single-minded in your service.
We ask this in the name of Jesus the Lord.
Amen.

Whatever prayer is used, it should offer thanks to God for the eucharist and look toward the effects the eucharist will have in our lives. The minister may wish to memorize the prayer.

Concluding Rites

The communion service ends with a simple blessing:

May the almighty and merciful God bless and protect us,
the Father, and the Son, and the Holy Spirit. Amen.

After the Service

After the service, clean the vessels you used to carry the blessed sacrament and make sure that no particles remain.

You may wish to continue to visit with the sick person, but be aware that he or she may need to rest, so take your lead from the sick person or the caregiver. Ask if the person would like you to return. Also, find out if the person has any needs that the parish can assist with.

After the Visit

If there is any of the blessed sacrament remaining, return it to the tabernacle in the church, or consume it in a reverent manner. Take a few moments to pray for the person and to give thanks to God for calling you to minister in this way. Be sure to tell the appropriate parish staff person of any needs that the person you visited may have. Some parishes have a register of communion visits that you will need to fill out. If you promised to bring anything to the person you visited on a future visit, make a note of it now so you will not forget.

When the Sick Person Is a Child

When visiting a sick child, it is very important that the special needs and situation of a child be considered. It may be most appropriate for the minister of communion to be someone with whom the child is already familiar. If none of the usual ministers of the parish knows the child, a parent or a friend from the parish might ask the pastor for permission to bring the child communion. If this is not possible, a parent might invite a communion minister to visit the child without bringing communion. That way, the child and the minister could become acquainted. The minister could then ask the child if he or she would like the minister to return sometime soon to give communion.

The communion visit described above might be shortened to accommodate the attention span of a young child. Remember to address the child directly rather than through the parent or other caregiver.

Further Formation

If you regularly visit the sick, you may wish to refer to some of the resources listed below. They are all available from Liturgy Training Publications.

Handbook for Ministers of Care by Genevieve Glen, osb, Marilyn Kofler, sp, and Kevin E. O'Connor. This book offers practical advice on being a minister of care, as well as a theology of sickness and suffering, and advice on caring for oneself while seeking to meet the needs of others.

Prayers for the Sick, Prayers for Later Years, Prayers with the Dying, and *Prayers for Caregivers.* These collections of scripture and prayer offer several options for praying with the sick or homebound, as well as prayers for those who care for them.

At Home with the Word. This annual publication contains the scripture readings for every Sunday of the year, a reflection on one of the readings, and seasonal psalms and prayers.

Questions for Reflection and Discussion

1. If you have never brought communion to the sick, is there anything about this part of being a communion minister that makes you uneasy?

2. If you have brought communion to the sick, what would you say to someone who is new to this ministry? Did you have any concerns when you first began? How did you resolve them?

Frequently Asked Questions

What should I do if I drop the bread or spill the wine? Accidents will happen on occasion. Ministers should be ready to deal with them quickly and discreetly. Panicky reactions will only tell the entire assembly that something has gone wrong and will be a distraction during the communion rite.

Spilled wine should be blotted up immediately with a purificator or towel. If a large amount has been spilled, wine-soaked towels should be placed in the sacrarium (the sink used for the purification of the sacred vessels). A clean towel should then be placed over the stain so that no one will step on the spot. A small spill may simply be covered with a purificator. Stain removal should wait until after Mass. Be sure to tell the sacristan that an accident has occurred.

In most cases, when a piece of consecrated bread is dropped while you are giving it to a communicant, the person will pick it up and consume it. If not, pick it up yourself. Consecrated bread that has fallen to the floor may be left on the altar, covered by a purificator, to be removed by the priest. Be sure that he is made aware of why the bread is there.

In some parishes, ministers of communion receive communion after everyone else. Why? The introduction to the sacramentary notes: "If communion is given under both kinds, the deacon ministers the chalice and is the last to drink from it." This is probably a sign that the deacon is one who is at the service of the assembly. This instruction was written before there were other ministers of communion. When laity were commissioned to serve as ministers of communion, some parishes extended this directive to them, both as a sign of service and to avoid delaying the communion of the people longer than necessary.

Ministers of communion should follow the procedure decided upon in their own parishes.

When I am ministering the cup, some people want to dip their host instead of taking the cup and drinking from it. Should I allow this? There are three permissible methods of receiving the blood of Christ in the Roman Catholic Church. The church's preferred method is that the individual drink from the cup. The words of Jesus instruct us to "take and drink."

The second method is intinction, that is, having the consecrated bread dipped in the wine before receiving. Should someone prefer to receive by intinction, that person should receive the communion bread in their hands, go to the minister of the cup, and hand the bread to the minister. The minister then dips the bread into the wine (no more than halfway), holds it over the cup and says, "The body and blood of Christ." After the person has responded, "Amen," the minister places the eucharist on the person's tongue. Both the minister and the communicant should be particularly careful when this procedure is followed. Wine can easily be spilled, and the consecrated bread may fall apart.

This procedure, although not the preferred method of distributing communion, should be explained to the assembly periodically. Individual communicants are not supposed to dip the bread into the wine themselves. However, it is not the minister's job to instruct or correct the communicant. If a person carrying the consecrated bread does wish to dip it in the cup, the minister should tip the cup to make it easier to do so. If this happens often, the minister should bring it to the attention of the priest or ministry coordinator.

The third method is very rarely used. One end of a small silver straw or pipe is dipped into the blood of Christ. The minister then covers the other end of the straw with a finger, moves the straw to the communicant's mouth and releases the wine by removing the finger. The straw is then placed in a dish of water. A clean straw is used for each communicant. This may seem quite strange to us, but it may be a useful option for giving communion to a person who is unable to eat or drink.

Should I say the name of the person to whom I am giving communion? The act of giving and receiving communion is an act of faith in the presence of Christ. The minister who says, "The body [blood] of Christ," is making a statement of faith to which the communicant gives assent by saying, "Amen." Nothing should dilute or diffuse that action.

The practice of saying the person's name when ministering communion to them comes from a desire to be hospitable and to recognize the bond each of us has with some people in the parish. Each and every person who comes to the Lord's table is equal and equally welcome. Each should be treated with the same respect and hospitality. While naming a friend, family member or well-known person in the parish may seem more hospitable to them, it may unintentionally make a person whose name is not said feel less welcome. Some parishes try to overcome this by asking each communicant to say their name to the minister, but this is artificial and distracts from the important act of giving and receiving communion.

Our primary bond at the celebration of the eucharist is our bond in the Lord Jesus. Through our baptism and through the eucharist, we are one in him. Everything else, even our name, is secondary. For this reason, ministers of communion are discouraged from naming individuals to whom they are ministering.

Should ministers of communion wash their hands before the communion rite? If the minister has blown his or her nose or helped a child do so, picked things up from the floor, or in some way soiled his or her hands since they were last washed, it is advisable that the minister go discreetly to the sacristy at the beginning of the sign of peace and wash his or her hands. Otherwise it is probably not necessary.

How should ministers of communion dress? In today's world, we rarely hear the phrase "Sunday best" anymore, but it is an excellent answer to this question. Even in parishes where casual attire is acceptable for the liturgy, ministers should take care that their appearance conveys the importance of their ministry.

"Sunday best" may mean different things in different areas. Culture, custom and climate will dictate what is appropriate in each parish. Those who direct the ministers of communion would do well to engage the group in discussion about appropriate dress. Most people will probably agree that shorts, t-shirts with slogans and insignia, exercise clothes, midriff-baring tops, very short skirts and sheer clothing are inappropriate. Sleeveless shirts on men, and shirts opened past the second button on both men and women, are probably also universally considered inappropriate. While hats are never appropriate on men in Catholic churches, sports-style caps are equally inappropriate on women. Each community should discuss the appropriateness of women's dress hats for ministers.

Ministers' purses, waist-packs, backpacks, beepers and other attachments are best left in the care of a family member or in the sacristy during the communion rite.

All ministers, men and women, should be careful about the amount of cologne they wear when serving. They should be particularly aware of any cologne or lotion that remains on the hands after it is applied. The taste of the cologne or lotion may be transferred to the bread that they handle.

Are some people "cup ministers" and other people "bread ministers"? There is no distinction among ministers of communion. A person who is commissioned to minister communion may distribute either the sacred bread or the wine. Parishes should not make any distinctions.

May a minister of communion go to the tabernacle? A minister of communion may go to the tabernacle when necessary, when the parish procedures indicate that they should, or when asked to do so by the priest, deacon or other appropriate person. Because the faithful should receive the bread consecrated at the Mass in which they participate, ministers of communion should not regularly need to go to the tabernacle at the beginning of the communion rite.

If I am a minister of communion, must I both serve at the liturgy and bring communion to the sick? While ministers of communion may perform both ministries, some prefer or are able to do only one or the other. You may wish to discuss this with your pastor or the person who coordinates the ministers. In some parishes, ministers who regularly bring communion to the sick are given special training and meet separately. They may also be called "ministers of care" or some other title to distinguish them from those who serve primarily at the liturgy.

If I agree to serve as a minister of communion, for how long am I committed to do so? Most parishes and dioceses have policies about how long a term of service for a communion minister is. In many cases, ministers are commissioned for three years. After that time, a minister may be commissioned for another term of service, usually after participating in a training update session. A minister may of course choose not to be recommissioned if they feel they can no longer carry out the commitment. Parishes should find ways to thank those who have served.

How are ministers of communion commissioned? The commissioning service for ministers of communion is a brief and simple order of prayer. It may take place during the Mass or at a special liturgy of the word. In either case, the candidates for this ministry come forward after the homily and are asked if they wish to undertake this ministry and if they promise to carry it out with care and reverence. A prayer of blessing is then prayed. This is one of the blessings that might be used:

> Gracious Lord,
> you nourish us with the body and blood of your Son,
> that we might have eternal life.
> Bless our brothers and sisters who have been chosen
> to give the bread of heaven and the cup of salvation
> to your faithful people.
> May the saving mysteries they distribute
> lead them to the joys of eternal life.
> We ask this through Christ our Lord. Amen.

Intercessions for the ministers are included in the general intercessions. If the commissioning takes place at Mass, the liturgy continues as usual; some of the new ministers may serve at communion time. If the commissioning takes place outside Mass, the service concludes with the Lord's Prayer and a blessing.

Appendix: Communion of the Sick

Introduction

Whoever eats this bread will live for ever.

71   [This rite is] for use when communion can be celebrated in the context of a liturgy of the word.

72   Priests with pastoral responsibilities should see to it that the sick or aged, even though not seriously ill or in danger of death, are given every opportunity to receive the eucharist frequently, even daily, especially during the Easter season. They may receive communion at any hour. Those who care for the sick may receive

communion with them, in accord with the usual norms. To provide frequent communion for the sick, it may be necessary to ensure that the community has a sufficient number of ministers of communion. The communion minister should wear attire appropriate to this ministry.

The sick person and others may help to plan the celebration, for example, by choosing the prayers and readings. Those making these choices should keep in mind the condition of the sick person. The readings and the homily should help those present to reach a deeper understanding of the mystery of human suffering in relation to the paschal mystery of Christ.

73 The faithful who are ill are deprived of their rightful and accustomed place in the eucharistic community. In bringing communion to them the minister of communion represents Christ and manifests faith and charity on behalf of the whole community toward those who cannot be present at the eucharist. For the sick the reception of communion is not only a privilege but also a sign of support and concern shown by the Christian community for its members who are ill.

The links between the community's eucharistic celebration, especially on the Lord's Day, and the communion of the sick are intimate and manifold. Besides remembering the sick in the general intercessions at Mass, those present should be reminded occasionally of the significance of communion in the lives of those who are ill: union with Christ in his struggle with evil, his prayer for the world, and his love for the Father, and union with the community from which they are separated.

The obligation to visit and comfort those who cannot take part in the eucharistic assembly may be clearly demonstrated by taking communion to them from the community's eucharistic celebration. This symbol of unity between the community and its sick members has the deepest significance on the Lord's Day, the special day of the eucharistic assembly.

74 When the eucharist is brought to the sick, it should be carried in a pyx or small closed container. Those who are with the

sick should be asked to prepare a table covered with a linen cloth upon which the blessed sacrament will be placed. Lighted candles are prepared and, where it is customary, a vessel of holy water. Care should be taken to make the occasion special and joyful.

Sick people who are unable to receive communion under the form of bread may receive it under the form of wine alone. If the wine is consecrated at a Mass not celebrated in the presence of the sick person, the blood of the Lord is kept in a properly covered vessel and is placed in the tabernacle after communion. The precious blood should be carried to the sick in a vessel which is closed in such a way as to eliminate all danger of spilling. If some of the precious blood remains, it should be consumed by the minister, who should also see to it that the vessel is properly purified.

75   If the sick wish to celebrate the sacrament of penance, it is preferable that the priest make himself available for this during a previous visit.

76   If it is necessary to celebrate the sacrament of penance during the rite of communion, it takes the place of the penitential rite.

Communion
in Ordinary
Circumstances

Introductory Rites

Greeting

81   *The minister greets the sick person and the others present.*
One of the following may be used:

A   The peace of the Lord be with you always.
     R. *And also with you.*

B   Peace be with you (this house) and with all who live here.
     R. *And also with you.*

C   The grace of our Lord Jesus Christ and the love of God and
     the fellowship of the Holy Spirit be with you all.
     R. *And also with you.*

D   The grace and peace of God our Father and the Lord Jesus
     Christ be with you.
     R. *And also with you.*

The minister then places the blessed sacrament on the table, and all join
in adoration.

Sprinkling with Holy Water

82   *If it seems desirable, the priest or deacon may sprinkle the sick*
person and those present with holy water. One of the following may be
used:

A   Let this water call to mind our baptism into Christ, who by
     his death and resurrection has redeemed us.

COMUNIÓN EN CIRCUNSTANCIAS ORDINARIAS

Ritos introductorios

Saludo

81   El ministro saluda a la persona enferma y a los presentes. Puede utilizar, para ello, una de las siguientes fórmulas:

A   La paz del Señor esté siempre con ustedes.
      R. *Y también contigo.*

B   La paz del Señor reine en esta casa y en todos los que en
      ella habitan.
      R. *Y también contigo.*

C   La gracia de nuestro Señor Jesucristo, el amor del Padre y
      la comunión del Espíritu Santo estén con todos ustedes.
      R. *Y también contigo.*

D   La gracia y la paz de Dios, nuestro Padre, y de Jesucristo,
      el Señor, estén con ustedes.
      R. *Y también contigo.*

Entonces el ministro coloca el Santísimo Sacramento en la mesa y todos juntos lo adoran.

Aspersión con agua bendita

82   Si parece conveniente, el sacerdote o el diácono rocía con agua bendita a la persona enferma y a todos los presentes. Se puede utilizar una de las siguientes fórmulas:

A   Que esta agua bendita nos recuerde
      el bautismo que recibimos
      y renueve nuestra fe en Cristo,
      que con su muerte y resurrección nos redimió.

B   Like a stream in parched land,
     may the grace of the Lord
     refresh our lives.

If the sacrament of penance is now celebrated, the penitential rite is omitted.

Penitential Rite

83   *The minister invites the sick person and all present to join in the penitential rite, using these or similar words:*

A   My brothers and sisters, to prepare ourselves for this celebration, let us call to mind our sins.

B   My brothers and sisters, let us turn with confidence to the Lord and ask his forgiveness for all our sins.

After a brief period of silence, the penitential rite continues, using one of the following:

A   Lord Jesus, you healed the sick:
     Lord, have mercy.
     R. *Lord, have mercy.*

     Lord Jesus, you forgave sinners:
     Christ, have mercy.
     R. *Christ, have mercy.*

     Lord Jesus, you give us yourself to heal us and bring us strength:
     Lord, have mercy.
     R. *Lord, have mercy.*

B   *All say:*
     I confess to almighty God,
     and to you, my brothers and sisters,
     that I have sinned through my own fault
         They strike their breast.
     in my thoughts and in my words,
     in what I have done,
     and in what I have failed to do;

B   Que la gracia del Señor
       nos dé la vida,
       como un río en medio del desierto.

Si tiene lugar aquí el sacramento de la penitencia, se omite el rito penitencial.

Rito penitencial

83   *El ministro invita a la persona enferma y a todos los presentes a participar en el rito penitencial, con estas u otras palabras parecidas:*

A   Hermanos y hermanas,
       para prepararnos a esta celebración,
       reconozcamos nuestros pecados.

B   Hermanos y hermanas,
       con toda nuestra confianza puesta en el Señor,
       pidámosle perdón por todos nuestros pecados.

Después de un breve momento de silencio, prosigue el rito penitencial con una de las siguientes fórmulas:

A   Señor Jesús, que curaste a los enfermos:
       Señor, ten piedad de nosotros.
       R. Señor, ten piedad de nosotros.

       Señor Jesús, que perdonaste a los pecadores:
       Cristo, ten piedad de nosostros.
       R. Cristo, ten piedad de nosostros.

       Señor Jesús, que te entregaste a la muerte
       para sanarnos y darnos fortaleza:
       Señor, ten piedad de nosotros.
       R. Señor, ten piedad de nosotros.

B   Yo confieso ante Dios todopoderoso
       y ante ustedes, hermanos,
       que he pecado mucho
       de pensamiento, palabra, obra y omisión;
       por mi culpa, por mi culpa, por mi gran culpa.
          Se golpean el pecho.

and I ask blessed Mary, ever virgin,
all the angels and saints,
and you, my brothers and sisters,
to pray for me to the Lord our God.

The minister concludes the penitential rite with the following:

May almighty God have mercy on us,
forgive us our sins,
and bring us to everlasting life.
R. Amen.

Liturgy of the Word

Reading

84   *The word of God is proclaimed by one of those present or by the minister. One of the following readings may be used:*

A   A reading from the holy gospel according to John   *6:51*

Jesus says:
"I myself am the living bread
come down from heaven.
If anyone eats this bread
he shall live forever;
the bread I will give
is my flesh, for the life of the world."

The Gospel of the Lord.

B   A reading from the holy gospel according to John 6:54 – 58

Jesus says:
"He who feeds on my flesh
and drinks my blood
has life eternal,
and I will raise him up on the last day.
For my flesh is real food
and my blood real drink.

Por eso ruego a Santa María, siempre Virgen,
a los ángeles, a los santos,
y a ustedes, hermanos,
que intercedan por mí ante Dios, nuestro Señor.

El ministro concluye el rito penitencial, diciendo:

El Señor todopoderoso tenga misericordia de nosotros,
perdone nuestros pecados
y nos lleve a la vida eterna.
R. *Amén*

Liturgia de la Palabra

Lectura

84   *Uno de los presentes o el ministro proclama la palabra de Dios.*

A   Lectura del santo Evangelio según san Juan   6, 51

Jesús dice:
"Yo soy el pan vivo que ha bajado del cielo;
el que coma de este pan vivirá para siempre.
Y el pan que yo les voy a dar a ustedes
es mi carne, para que el mundo tenga vida".

Palabra del Señor.

B   Lectura del santo Evangelio según san Juan   6, 54–58

Jesús dice:
"El que come mi carne y bebe mi sangre
tiene vida eterna y yo lo resucitaré el último día.
Mi carne es verdadera comida
y mi sangre es verdadera bebida.
El que come mi carne y bebe mi sangre
permanence en mí y yo en él.
Como el Padre, que me ha enviado,
posee la vida y yo vivo por él,
así también el que me come vivirá por mí.

The man who feeds on my flesh
and drinks my blood
remains in me, and I in him.
Just as the Father who has life sent me
and I have life because of the Father,
so the man who feeds on me
will have life because of me.
This is the bread that came down from heaven.
Unlike your ancestors who ate and died nonetheless,
the man who feeds on this bread shall live forever."

The Gospel of the Lord.

C   A reading from the holy gospel according to John   *14:6*

Jesus says:
"I am the way, and the truth, and the life;
no one comes to the Father but through me."

The Gospel of the Lord.

D   A reading from the holy gospel according to John   *15:5*

Jesus says:
"I am the vine, you are the branches.
He who lives in me and I in him,
will produce abundantly,
for apart from me you can do nothing."

The Gospel of the Lord.

E   A reading from the first letter of John   *4:16*

We have come to know and to believe
in the love God has for us.
God is love,
and he who abides in love
abides in God,
and God in him.

The Word of the Lord.

Este es el pan que ha bajado del cielo;
no es como el maná que comieron
los padres de ustedes, pues murieron.
El que come de este pan vivirá para siempre".

Palabra del Señor.

C   Lectura del santo Evangelio según san Juan   *14, 6*

Jesús dice:
"Yo soy el camino, la verdad y la vida.
Nadie va al Padre, sí no es por mí".

Palabra del Señor.

D   Lectura del santo Evangelio según san Juan   *15, 5*

Jesús dice:
"Yo soy la vid,
ustedes los sarmientos;
el que permanece en mí y yo en él,
ése da fruto abundante,
porque sin mí nada pueden hacer ustedes".

Palabra del Señor.

E   Lectura de la primera carta del apóstol san Juan   *4, 16*

Queridos hijos:
Nosotros hemos conocido el amor que Dios nos tiene
y hemos creído en ese amor.
Dios es amor y quien permanece en el amor,
permanece en Dios, y Dios en él.

Palabra de Dios.

Response

85   *A brief period of silence may be observed after the reading of the word of God.*

The minister may then give a brief explanation of the reading, applying it to the needs of the sick person and those who are looking after him or her.

General Intercessions

86   *The general intercessions may be said. With a brief introduction the minister invites all those present to pray. After the intentions the minister says the concluding prayer. It is desirable that the intentions be announced by someone other than the minister.*

Liturgy of Holy Communion

The Lord's Prayer

87   *The minister introduces the Lord's Prayer in these or similar words:*

A   Now let us pray as Christ the Lord has taught us:

B   And now let us pray with confidence as Christ our Lord commanded:

All say:
Our Father . . .

Communion

88   *The minister shows the eucharistic bread to those present, saying:*

A   This is the bread of life.
Taste and see that the Lord is good.

Respuesta a la Palabra

85   *Se puede guardar un breve espacio de silencio, después de la lectura de la palabra de Dios.*

El ministro podrá explicar brevemente la lectura y aplicarla a las necesidades de la persona enferma y de los que cuidan de ella.

Preces

86   *Se pueden enunciar las peticiones generales. Mediante una breve introducción, el ministro invita a todos a orar. Después de las intenciones, el ministro recita la oración conclusiva. Es recomendable que una persona distinta del ministro pronuncie las intenciones.*

Liturgia de la comunión

Padrenuestro

87   *El ministro introduce la oración del Señor con éstas u otras palabras similares:*

A   Oremos confiadamente al Padre con las palabras
    que nos enseñó nuestro Salvador:

B   Fieles a la recomendación del Salvador,
    y siguiendo su divina enseñanza,
    nos atrevemos a decir:

   Todos dicen:
   Padre nuestro . . .

Comunión

88   *El ministro presenta el pan eucarístico a los presentes, con estas palabras:*

A   Este es el pan de la vida.
    Prueben y vean qué bueno es el Señor.

B   This is the Lamb of God
     who takes away the sins of the world.
     Happy are those who are called to his supper.

The sick person and all who are to receive communion say:
Lord, I am not worthy to receive you,
but only say the word and I shall be healed.

The minister goes to the sick person and, showing the blessed sacrament, says:
The body of Christ.
The sick person answers: "Amen," and receives communion.

Then the minister says:
The blood of Christ.
The sick person answers: "Amen," and receives communion.

Others present who wish to receive communion then do so in the usual way. After the conclusion of the rite, the minister cleanses the vessel as usual.

Silent Prayer

89   *Then a period of silence may be observed.*

Prayer after Communion

90   *The minister says a concluding prayer. One of the following may be used:*

     Let us pray.

Pause for silent prayer, if this has not preceded.

A   God our Father,
     you have called us to share the one bread and one cup
     and so become one in Christ.

     Help us to live in him
     that we may bear fruit,
     rejoicing that he has redeemed the world.

     We ask this through Christ our Lord.
     R. Amen.

B   Este es el Cordero de Dios
que quita el pecado del mundo.
¡Dichosos los invitados a la cena del Señor!

La persona enferma y todos los que vayan a recibir la comunión dicen:
Señor, yo no soy digno de que vengas a mí,
pero una palabra tuya bastará para sanarme.

El ministro se acerca a la persona enferma y presentándole la sagrada forma, dice:
El Cuerpo de Cristo.
La persona enferma responde: "Amén" y recibe la comunión.

Enseguida el ministro dice:
La Sangre de Cristo.
La persona enferma responde: "Amén" y recibe la comunión.

Si algunas otras personas presentes quieren comulgar, lo hacen en la forma acostumbrada. Terminado el rito, el ministro purifica los vasos sagrados, como de costumbre.

Oración en silenco

89   *Se puede orar aquí en silencio.*

Oración después de la comunión

90   *El ministro reza la oración conclusiva. Puede utilizarse una de las siguientes.*

Oremos.

Pausa para orar en silencio, si no se ha hecho anteriormente.

A   Señor y Padre nuestro,
que nos has llamado a participar
del mismo pan y del mismo vino,
para vivir así unidos a Cristo,
ayúndanos a vivir unidos a él,
para que produzcamos fruto,
experimentando el gozo de su redención.
Por Cristo, nuestro Señor.
R. *Amén.*

B   All-powerful God,
    we thank you for the nourishment you give us
    through your holy gift.

    Pour out your Spirit upon us
    and in the strength of this food from heaven
    keep us single-minded in your service.

    We ask this in the name of Jesus the Lord.
    R. Amen.

C   All-powerful and ever-living God,
    may the body and blood of Christ your Son
    be for our brother/sister N.
    a lasting remedy for body and soul.

    We ask this through Christ our Lord.
    R. Amen.

Concluding Rite

Blessing

91   *The priest or deacon blesses the sick person and the others present, using one of the following blessings. If, however, any of the blessed sacrament remains, he may bless the sick person by making a sign of the cross with the blessed sacrament, in silence.*

A   May God the Father bless you.
    R. Amen.
    May God the Son heal you.
    R. Amen.
    May God the Holy Spirit enlighten you.
    R. Amen.
    May almighty God bless you,
    the Father, and the Son, + and the Holy Spirit.
    R. Amen.

B   Señor Dios todopoderoso,
     te damos gracias por este don sagrado
     que constituye nuestro alimento.
     Derrama en nosotros tu Santo Espíritu
     y con el vigor que nos comunica este alimento celestial,
     haz que nos entreguemos de corazón a tu servicio.
     Te lo pedimos por Cristo, nuestro Señor.
     R. Amen.

C   [Señor, Padre santo, Dios todopoderoso y eterno,
     te suplicamos humildemente que el Cuerpo santísimo
     (y la Sangre preciosa) de tu Hijo Jesucristo,
     que nuestros hermanos y hermanas han recibido,
     les sirva para bien de su alma y de su cuerpo
     y como remedio para alcanzar la vida eterna.
     Por Cristo, nuestro Señor.
     R. Amen.]

Rito conclusivo

Bendición

91   *El sacerdote o el diácono bendice a la persona enferma y a los presentes, utilizando para ello, una de las siguientes fórmulas. Pero, en el caso de que hayan quedado algunas formas consagradas, puede bendecir al enfermo, haciendo, en silencio, la señal de la cruz con el Santísimo Sacramento.*

A   Que Dios Padre te bendiga.
     R. Amén.
     Que Dios Hijo te cure.
     R. Amén.
     Que Dios Espíritu Santo te ilumine.
     R. Amén.

B   May the Lord be with you to protect you.
R. *Amen.*
May he guide you and give you strength.
R. *Amen.*
May he watch over you, keep you in his care,
and bless you with his peace.
R. *Amen.*
May almighty God bless you,
the Father, and the Son, + and the Holy Spirit.
R. *Amen.*

C   May the blessing of almighty God,
the Father, and the Son, + and the Holy Spirit,
come upon you and remain with you for ever.
R. *Amen.*

A minister who is not a priest or deacon invokes God's blessing and makes the sign of the cross on himself or herself, while saying:

A   May the Lord bless us,
protect us from all evil,
and bring us to everlasting life.
R. *Amen.*

B   May the almighty and merciful God bless and protect us,
the Father, and the Son, and the Holy Spirit.
R. *Amen.*

Que te bendiga Dios todopoderoso,
Padre, Hijo + y Espíritu Santo.
R. Amén.

B Que el Señor esté contigo para protegerte.
R. Amén.
Que el Señor te guíe y te dé fortaleza.
R. Amén.
Que el Señor te cuide, te defienda y te bendiga con su paz.
R. Amén.
Que te bendiga Dios todopoderoso,
Padre, Hijo + y Espíritu Santo.
R. Amén.

C La bendición de Dios todopoderoso,
Padre, Hijo + y Espíritu Santo,
descienda sobre ti (ustedes)
y permanezca para siempre.
R. Amén.

Si el ministro no es sacerdote ni diácono, invoca la bendición de Dios y hace sobre sí mismo(a) la señal de la cruz, diciendo:

A Que el Señor nos bendiga,
nos libre de todo mal
y nos lleve a la vida eterna.
R. Amén

B Que nos bendiga y nos proteja
Dios todopoderoso y lleno de misericordia,
Padre, Hijo y Espíritu Santo.
R. Amén